EARLY INTERMEDIATE

More Christmas Creations

9 SEASONAL PIANO SOLOS
Arranged by RANDALL HARTSELL

ISBN 978-1-4584-1086-3

WILLIS MUSIC

EXCLUSIVELY DISTRIBUTED BY

HAL•LEONARD®
CORPORATION

7777 W. BLUEMOUND RD. P.O. BOX 13819 MILWAUKEE, WI 53213

Visit Hal Leonard Online at
www.halleonard.com

FOREWORD

I love arranging well-known compositions for the piano.
Over the years, I have arranged many traditional Christmas
carols, from elementary to more advanced levels. This
book contains my first arrangements from the "pop" genre
of Christmas music, and I must say that I enjoyed every
moment of the process.

As an arranger, I hear familiar music in a fresh and creative
way, and I try to add new life to old favorite tunes. These
arrangements can sound energetic and showy. Some have
flowing, expressive lines. Yet, all are easy to learn!

Use this book for a lively Christmas recital. Share the music
with friends and give yourself an early Christmas present...
the gift of music. Enjoy!

Randall Hartsell

for Chandler Schramm

CONTENTS

Christmas Time Is Here

from A CHARLIE BROWN CHRISTMAS

Words by Lee Mendelson
Music by Vince Guaraldi
Arranged by Randall Hartsell

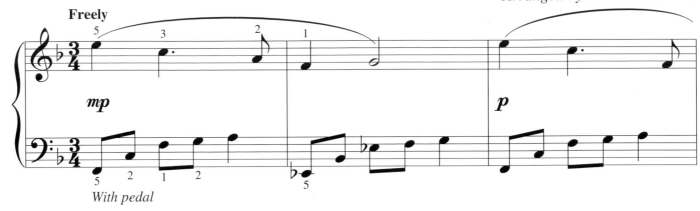

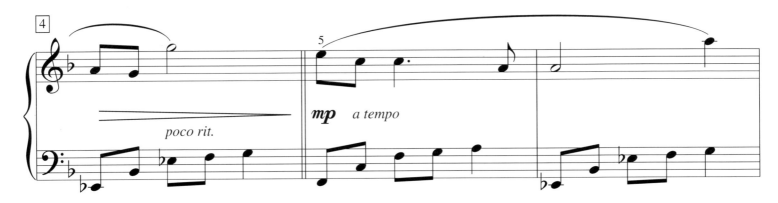

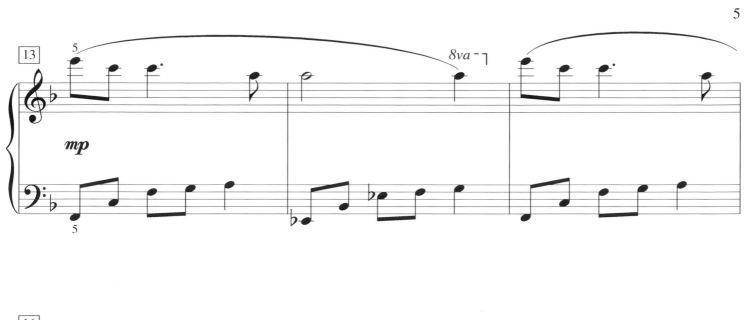

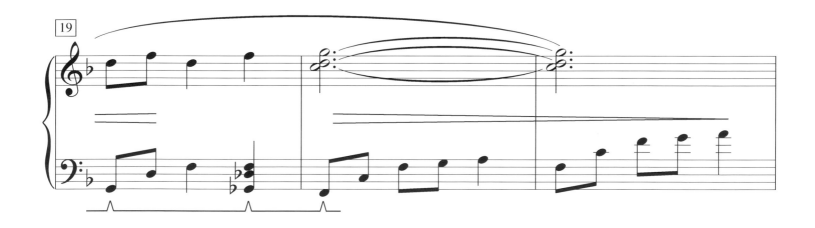

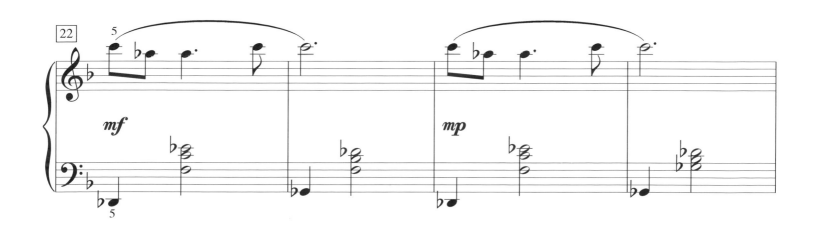

Do You Hear What I Hear

Words and Music by Noel Regney
and Gloria Shayne
Arranged by Randall Hartsell

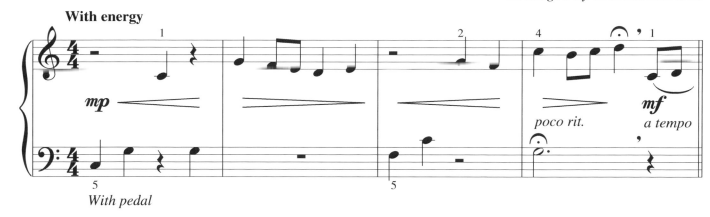

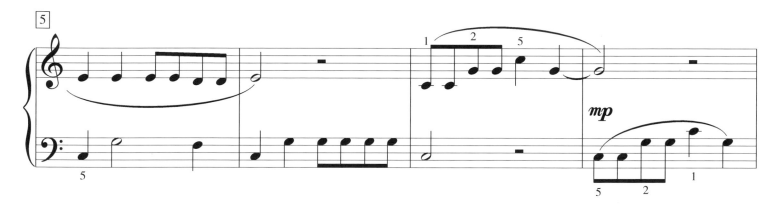

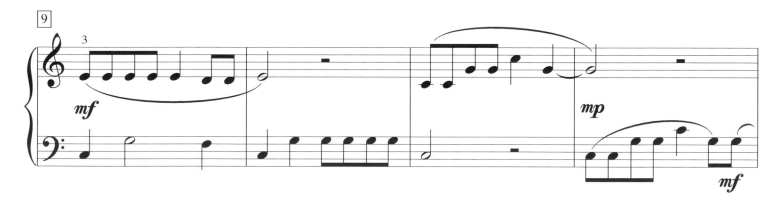

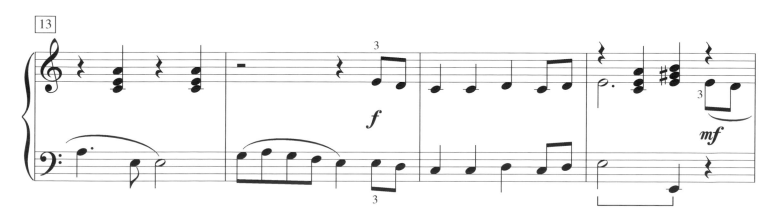

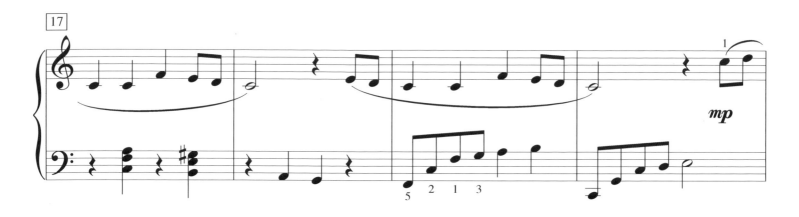

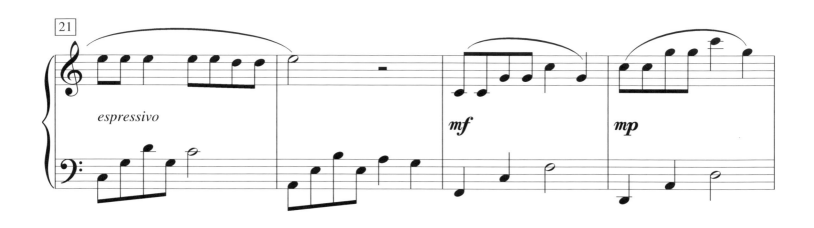

Here Comes Santa Claus
(Right Down Santa Claus Lane)

Words and Music by Gene Autry
and Oakley Haldeman
Arranged by Randall Hartsell

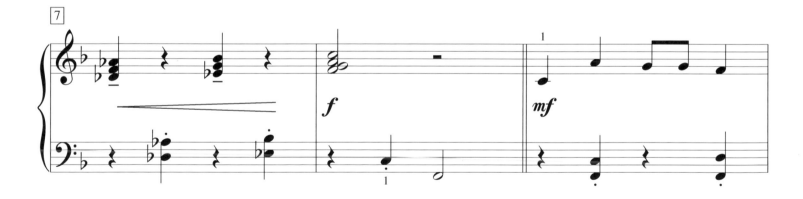

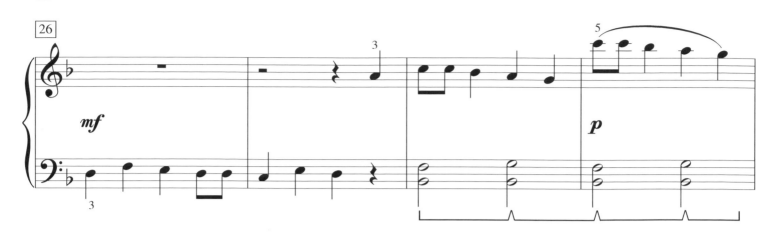

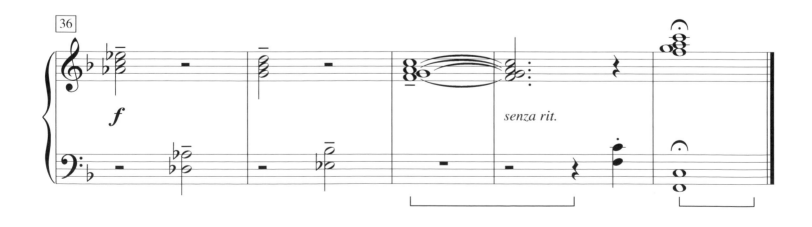

A Holly Jolly Christmas

Music and Lyrics by Johnny Marks
Arranged by Randall Hartsell

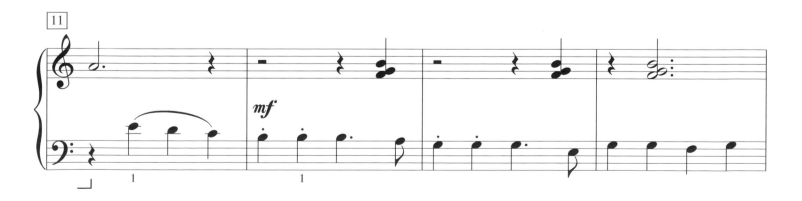

14

I'll Be Home for Christmas

Words and Music by Kim Gannon
and Walter Kent
Arranged by Randall Hartsell

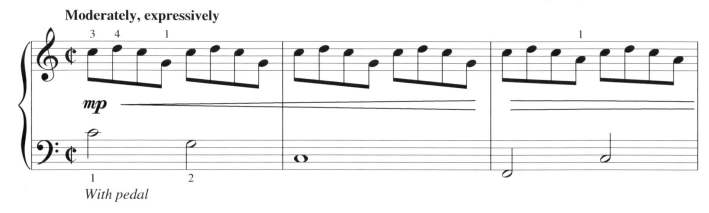

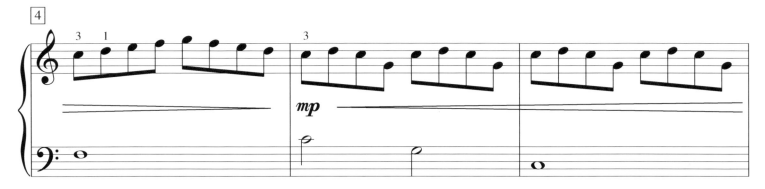

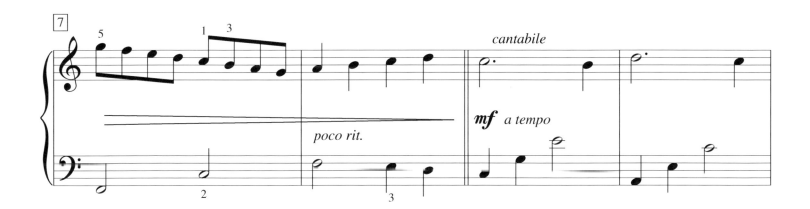

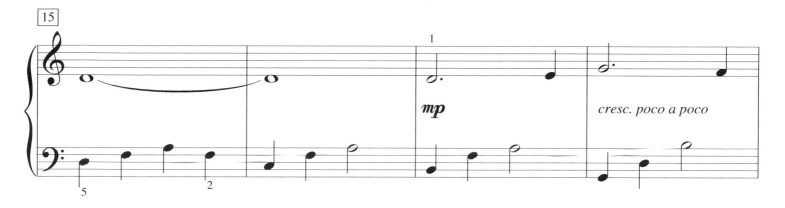

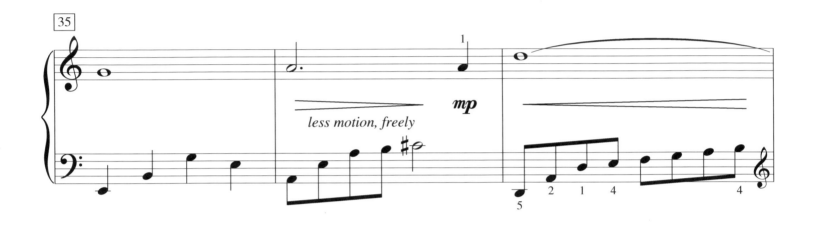

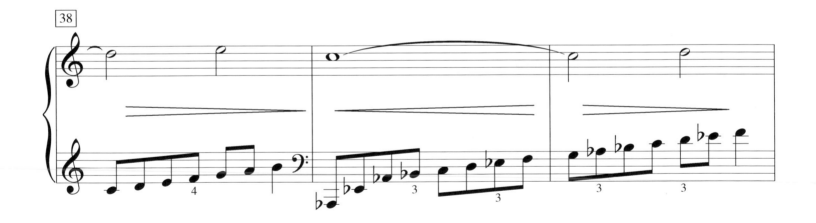

Let It Snow! Let It Snow! Let It Snow!

Words by Sammy Cahn
Music by Jule Styne
Arranged by Randall Hartsell

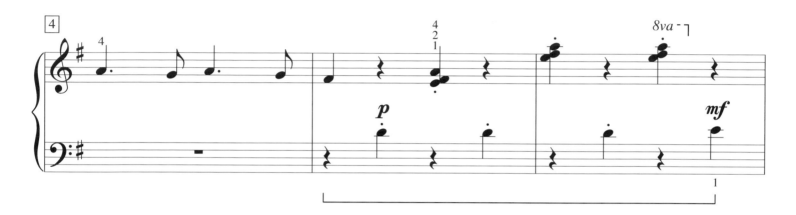

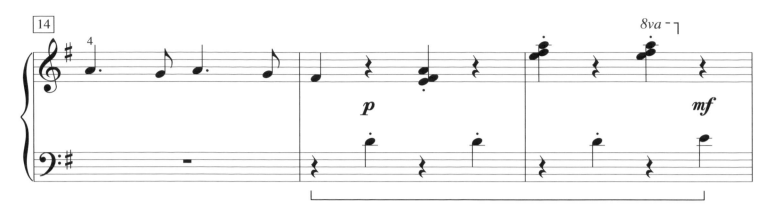

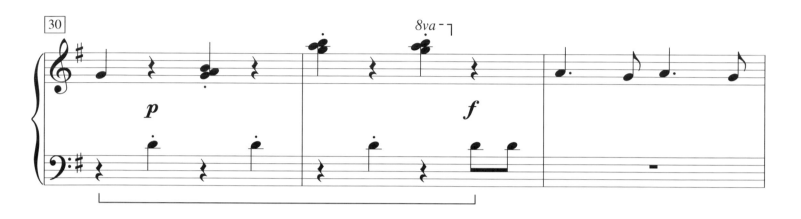

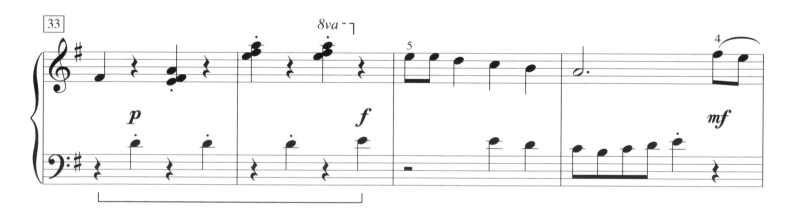

Rudolph the Red-Nosed Reindeer

Music and Lyrics by Johnny Marks
Arranged by Randall Hartsell

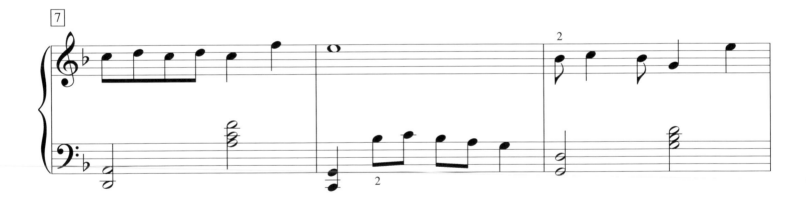

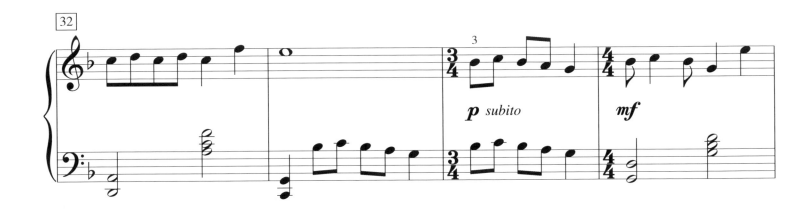

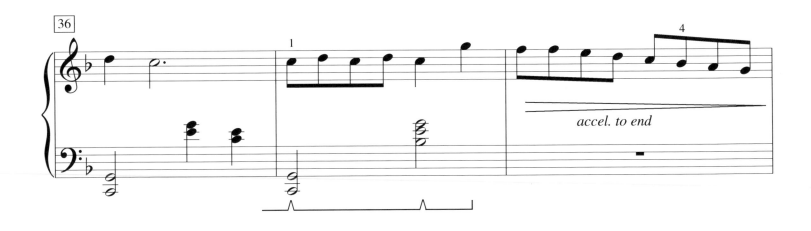

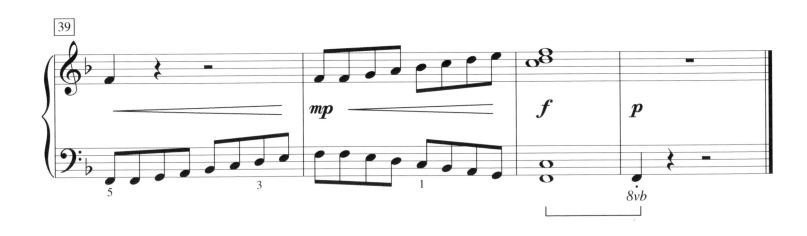

Silver Bells

from the Paramount Picture THE LEMON DROP KID

Words and Music by Jay Livingston
and Ray Evans
Arranged by Randall Hartsell

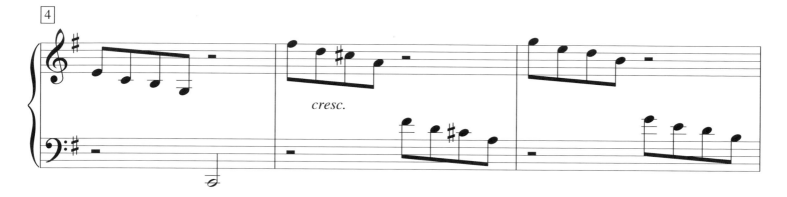

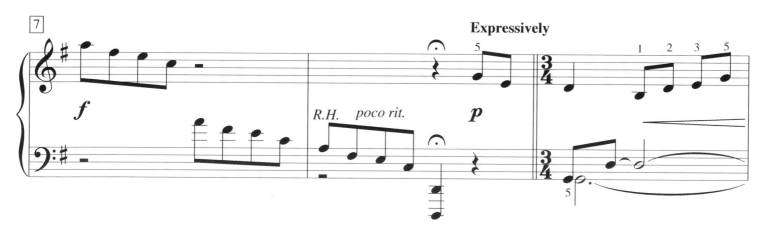

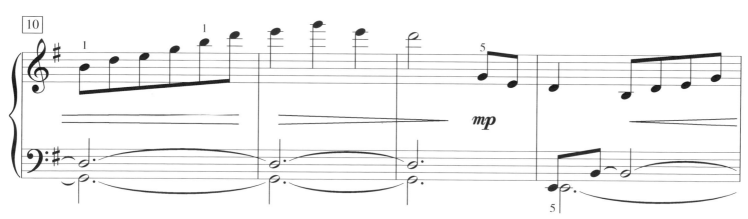

Wonderful Christmastime

Words and Music by Paul McCartney
Arranged by Randall Hartsell

Brightly, with a lilt

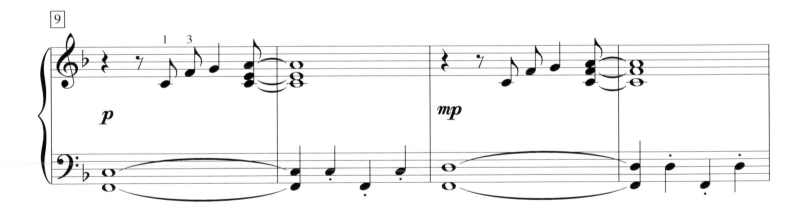

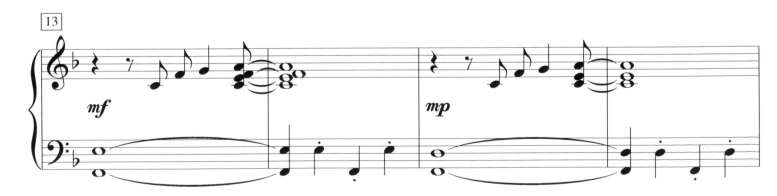

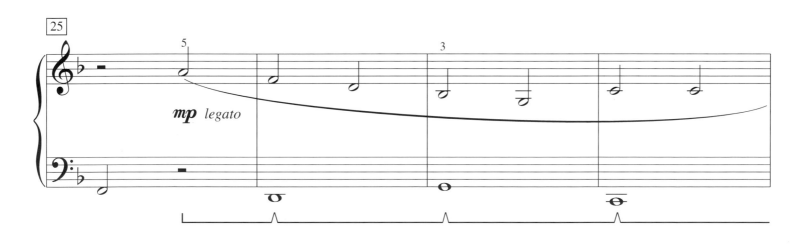

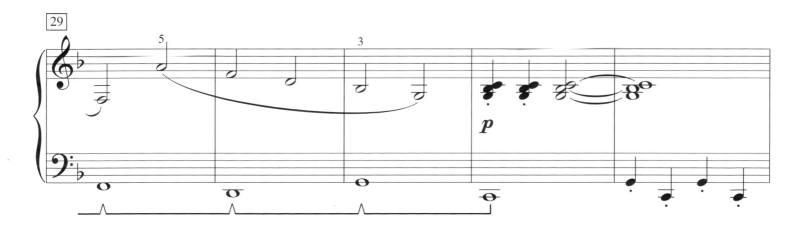

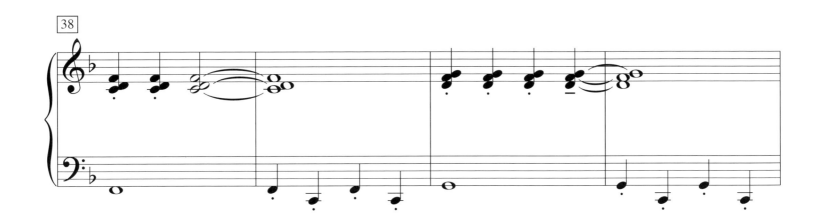

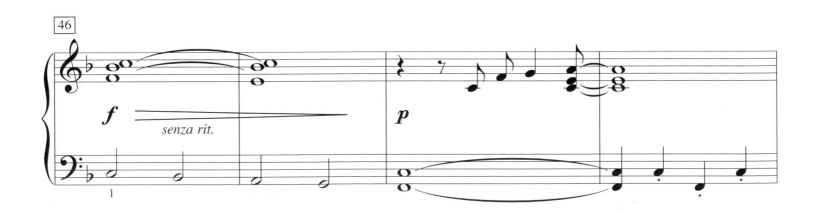

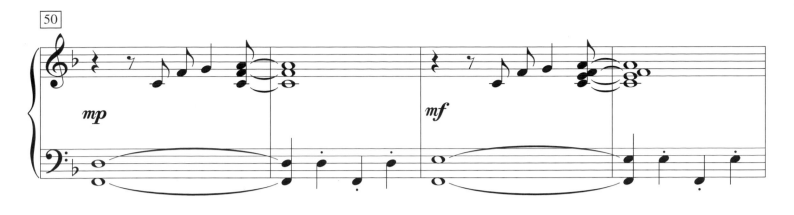

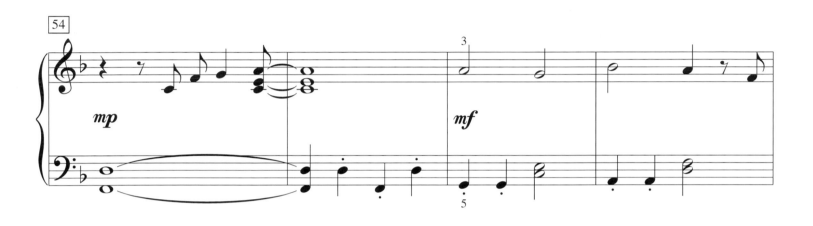

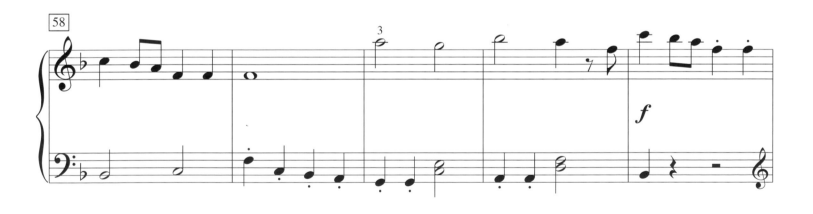

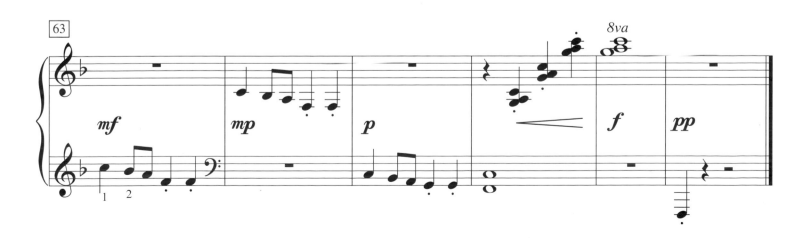

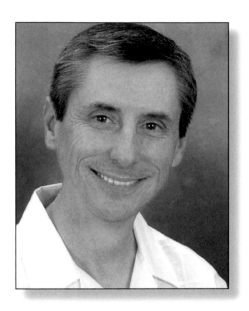

BIOGRAPHY

RANDALL HARTSELL is a composer, pianist/organist, clinician and teacher from Charlotte, North Carolina. Mr. Hartsell is particularly known for his lyrical and melodic compositional style, and consistently aims to write pieces that students will love to play and teachers will love to teach! He currently operates a private studio in the Charlotte area.

Mr. Hartsell is a graduate of East Carolina University, where he majored in piano pedagogy and performance, and was previously on the faculty of the school of music at the University of North Carolina (Charlotte). He has well over 100 publications in print, and has been featured as a commissioned composer in *Clavier* magazine.

Visit **www.halleonard.com** for more works by Randall Hartsell.